POWER UP

Unless otherwise noted, scripture quotations are taken from the New King James Version®. Copyright © 1982 by Thomas Nelson. Used by permission. All rights reserved.

Scripture quotations marked KJV are taken from the King James Version®. Public domain.

Scripture quotations marked NCV are taken from the New Century Version®. Copyright © 2005 by Thomas Nelson. Used by permission. All rights reserved.

Scripture quotations marked NIV are taken from the Holy Bible, New International Version®, NIV®. Copyright © 1973, 1978, 1984, 2011 by Biblica, Inc.™ Used by permission of Zondervan. All rights reserved worldwide. www.zondervan.com The "NIV" and "New International Version" are trademarks registered in the United States Patent and Trademark Office by Biblica, Inc.™

ISBN: 978-1-963492-00-2

Created and assembled for Joel Osteen Ministries by
Breakfast for Seven
breakfastforseven.com

Printed in the United States of America.

For additional resources by Joel Osteen, visit JoelOsteen.com

POWER UP

A **21-Day** Action Plan to
Transformative Thinking

JOEL OSTEEN

CONTENTS

MY HEALTH

MY FINANCES

SCRIPTURES AT A GLANCE

BE CAREFUL WHAT YOU THINK, BECAUSE YOUR THOUGHTS RUN YOUR LIFE.

PROVERBS 4:23 (NCV)

INTRODUCTION

The way you think will determine the way you live!

So, let me ask you: when was the last time you thought about your thoughts? Proverbs 4:23 says, *Be careful what you think, because your thoughts run your life* (NCV).

It is common for people to let their thoughts run the show. People say to me, "Joel, I want to stop being distracted by every thought that comes to mind."

As a child of the Most High God, you were made for more than that. You want to let your thinking become powerful, focusing on the promises in His Word. To do that, you've got to make a choice — a choice to think about things that are true, right, and life-giving!

In *Power Up: A 21-Day Action Plan to Transformative Thinking*, I'm going to help you discover how to:

- Shift out of unconscious, habitual thinking.
- Hear what the Lord is saying to your spirit through His Word.
- Live with more peace and confidence as He reveals Himself through your newfound awareness.
- Experience the fruit of a powerful thought life.

Are you ready to power up your life with can-do thoughts? Abundant thoughts? Favor-filled thoughts?

It's time to fuel your future with God-first thinking!

**POWER UP
YOUR THOUGHTS . . .**

POWER UP
YOUR LIFE!

1

Right Thinking:

I CHOOSE HOPE OVER WORRY, FAITH OVER FEAR.

Wrong Thinking:

I NEVER GET A BREAK FROM WORRYING ABOUT MY TROUBLES.

"Therefore I say to you, do not worry about your life, what you will eat or what you will drink; nor about your body, what you will put on. Is not life more than food and the body more than clothing?"

MATTHEW 6:25

I CHOOSE HOPE OVER WORRY, FAITH OVER FEAR

E very day we can choose to dwell in worry or to embrace hope. It's easy to let fear grip our hearts, to let anxiety cloud our minds, but that is not the lives we are called to live. Instead, we are called to live lives of faith, trusting in the goodness of God and His plans for us.

When we choose hope over worry, we are aligning our hearts with the promises of God. We are declaring that no matter what challenges come our way, we believe that God is greater, and He is working all things together for our good. It's a mindset shift from focusing on our problems to focusing on the power of God to overcome them.

The Bible reminds us in Proverbs 12:25, *Anxiety in the heart of a man causes depression, but a good word makes it glad.* This verse highlights the destructive nature of worry and anxiety. When we allow ourselves to be consumed by fear, it leads to despair and hopelessness. But when we choose to speak words of faith and hope, it brings joy and gladness to our hearts.

In Matthew 6:25, Jesus Himself instructs us, *"Therefore I say to you, do not worry about your life, what you will eat or what you will drink; nor about your body, what you will put on. Is not life more than food and the body more than clothing?"* These words serve as a gentle reminder that God is our provider. He knows our needs even before we ask, and He promises to take care of us.

When we meditate on these truths and choose to trust in God's provision, it transforms our perspectives. Instead of dwelling on our troubles and worrying about tomorrow, we can rest in the assurance that God is in control. We can release our fears and anxieties into His capable hands, knowing that He will never leave us nor forsake us.

Second Timothy 1:7 says, *For God has not given us a spirit of fear, but of power and of love and of a sound mind.* The Amplified Bible adds *"personal discipline."* In other words, we're not going to overcome fear and live powerful, victorious lives if we're not disciplined in our thought lives. The battleground is not out there in the world; it's right between our ears! Your mind is the Enemy's bull's-eye. He knows that if he can infiltrate and control your thoughts, he can dictate the course of your life.

So, today, I encourage you: refuse to entertain thoughts that do not align with God's truth and promises for your life. It's a decision that we must make daily, sometimes moment by moment. It requires

Instead of dwelling on our troubles and worrying about tomorrow, we can rest in the assurance that God is in control.

surrendering our fears to God and allowing His peace to fill our hearts.

Make a conscious choice to think thoughts of hope and faith. Cast aside worry and fear, knowing that we serve a God who is faithful. As we embrace this mind-set shift, may we experience the joy and freedom that comes from trusting in Him completely.

Refuse to entertain thoughts that do not align with God's truth and promises for your life.

Power Up✝

"Blessed is the man who trusts in the LORD, and whose hope is the LORD. For he shall be like a tree planted by the waters, which spreads out its roots by the river, and will not fear when heat comes; but its leaf will be green, and will not be anxious in the year of drought, nor will cease from yielding fruit."
JEREMIAH 17:7–8

"Look at the birds of the air, for they neither sow nor reap nor gather into barns; yet your heavenly Father feeds them. Are you not of more value than they?"
MATTHEW 6:26

"Do not labor for the food which perishes, but for the food which endures to everlasting life, which the Son of Man will give you, because God the Father has set His seal on Him."
JOHN 6:27

Let your conduct be without covetousness; be content with such things as you have. For He Himself has said, "I will never leave you nor forsake you."
HEBREWS 13:5

Anxiety in the heart of a man causes depression, but a good word makes it glad.
PROVERBS 12:25

Right Thinking:

I KNOW THE LORD IS MAKING A WAY FOR ME EVEN WHEN THERE SEEMS TO BE NO WAY.

Wrong Thinking:

I DON'T THINK I CAN TAKE ANY MORE; I'M READY TO GIVE UP.

But those who wait on the LORD shall renew their strength; they shall mount up with wings like eagles, they shall run and not be weary, they shall walk and not faint.

ISAIAH 40:31

THE LORD IS MAKING A WAY FOR ME

In our fast-paced world, waiting often gets a bad rap. We tend to view it as a period of stagnation, a time when nothing seems to be happening. We feel overwhelmed when the weight of our burdens threatens to crush our spirits. In those moments, it's easy to entertain thoughts of giving up, to believe that there's no way out of the predicament. But as believers, we are called to think differently. We are called to hold on to the unwavering belief that God is always making a way for us, even when it seems impossible.

The Bible reminds us in Isaiah 40:31, *But those who wait on the LORD shall renew their strength; they shall mount up with wings like eagles, they shall run and not be weary, they shall walk and not faint.* This verse serves as a powerful reassurance that God is our source of strength and endurance. When we wait on Him, when we trust in His timing and His ways, He renews our strength beyond measure. Like eagles soaring high above the storm, we are lifted above our circumstances and given the energy to press on.

It's essential to understand that waiting on the Lord doesn't mean sitting idly by. It's an active posture of faith and trust. It's about surrendering our timelines and expectations to God and allowing Him to work in His perfect timing. As we wait, we continue to move forward in obedience, knowing that God is orchestrating every detail of our lives for our good. While we're eager for the destination, God is at work within us every step of the way — molding us, refining us, preparing us for what's ahead. When you grasp this truth, you realize that waiting isn't a sign of God forgetting about you or abandoning His plans for your life. No, it's all part of His process. When you embrace that perspective, you can walk in faith, knowing He will lead you exactly where you're meant to be.

We are called to hold on to the unwavering belief that God is always making a way for us.

Take David, for example. After the prophet Samuel anointed him as the next king, did David go straight to the throne? No. He waited thirteen years before he finally took his place as king. God could have fast-tracked him, but David wasn't ready. He needed that time of testing, of growth, to develop into the leader God intended him to be.

We live in a society that craves instant gratification, but let me remind you: we serve a Crock-Pot God, not a microwave God. You can't rush maturity, preparation, or growth. It's in the waiting that God shapes you, strengthens you, and equips you for the destiny He has ordained.

When we choose to think thoughts of faith and confidence in God's provision and timing, it changes our perspectives. Instead of focusing on the impossibilities, we fix our eyes on the One who holds all things together. We remind ourselves of His faithfulness in the past and trust that He will come through for us once again. In due time, He will bring forth the fullness of His promises.

I encourage you today to replace thoughts of doubt and despair with thoughts of hope and trust in God's unfailing love. Remember that He is always making a way for you, even in the darkest of times. Take comfort in knowing that His plans for you are good, and He will never leave you nor forsake you.

As you wait on the Lord, I pray you experience a renewed sense of strength and perseverance.

Take comfort in knowing that His plans for you are good.

Power Up✝

"Take My yoke upon you and learn from Me, for I am gentle and lowly in heart, and you will find rest for your souls."
MATTHEW 11:29

I wait for the LORD, my soul waits, and in His word I do hope.
PSALM 130:5

Let us hold fast the confession of our hope without wavering, for He Who promised is faithful.
HEBREWS 10:23

The LORD is good to those who wait for Him, to the soul who seeks Him.
LAMENTATIONS 3:25

Rest in the LORD, and wait patiently for Him; do not fret because of him who prospers in his way, because of the man who brings wicked schemes to pass. Cease from anger, and forsake wrath; do not fret — it only causes harm. For evildoers shall be cut off; but those who wait on the LORD, they shall inherit the earth.
PSALM 37:7–9

Right Thinking:

GOD HAS FREEDOM AND BREAKTHROUGH IN STORE FOR ME.

Wrong Thinking:

THERE'S NO WAY I CAN OVERCOME THIS ADDICTION.

"My grace is sufficient for you, for My strength is made perfect in weakness."

2 CORINTHIANS 12:9

GOD HAS FREEDOM AND BREAKTHROUGH FOR ME

Let me remind you of a comforting truth today: God knew every mistake, every stumble, every failure before you even took your first breath. Whether it's addiction, fear, doubt, or any other stronghold, it's easy to feel overwhelmed and powerless. But here's the beautiful part: He's already orchestrated your restoration, your second chance, your comeback story.

Think of Jonah. When God instructed him to go to Nineveh, Jonah chose to head in the opposite direction. He went completely against what he knew he was supposed to do. Maybe you feel like you've veered off course, like you've missed your destiny. But if only you could grasp the lengths God has gone to bring you back! God has freedom and breakthrough in store for you, even in the midst of your greatest challenges.

There is no distance too great, no pit too deep, where God cannot reach you. Even if you've made choices you regret, God's love for you remains. Just like Jonah, you can still step into the fullness of who you were created to be. God's calling on your life hasn't been ruined because of a detour.

The Bible says in 2 Corinthians 12:9, *"My grace is sufficient for you, for My strength is made perfect in weakness."* Let this remind you that you don't have to rely on your own strength to overcome obstacles. Instead, lean on the grace of God, knowing that His power is made perfect in your moment of weakness. It's in your moments of greatest struggle that God's strength shines through, enabling you to experience true freedom and breakthrough.

James 4:10 says, *Humble yourselves in the sight of the Lord, and He will lift you up.* This verse reminds us of the importance of humility and surrender in experiencing God's transformative work in our lives. When we humble ourselves before God, acknowledging our need for His help and guidance, He lifts us up and empowers us to overcome.

There is no distance too great, no pit too deep, where God cannot reach you.

God's promise of freedom and breakthrough isn't just wishful thinking. It's a reality that we can claim through faith and obedience. When we choose to think thoughts of victory and breakthrough, we align our minds with God's promises, opening ourselves up to receive His blessings in abundance.

Instead of dwelling on thoughts of defeat and hopelessness, fix your eyes on the One who is able to do immeasurably more than you could ever ask or imagine. Declare with confidence that God has freedom and breakthrough in store.

If you're struggling with addiction, know that God has the power to set you free and break every chain that binds you. If you're facing fear or doubt, know that God is greater than any obstacle standing in your way. Whatever battles you may be fighting, remember that God is fighting for you, and He has already secured the victory.

Remember, His calling on your life hasn't been ruined because of mistakes, because of a detour. So, lift your head high. Your comeback story is already written, and it's going to be nothing short of extraordinary. You're going to see breakthrough — not where you're a little better, partially free, or almost free — you'll be unquestionably, abundantly, and totally free. Choose to believe that's what your future holds.

Whatever battles you may be fighting, remember that God is fighting for you, and He has already secured the victory.

Power Up✝

Let the words of my mouth and the meditation of my heart be acceptable in Your sight, O LORD, my strength and my Redeemer.
PSALM 19:14

"I have been crucified with Christ; it is no longer I who live, but Christ lives in me; and the life which I now live in the flesh I live by faith in the Son of God, who loved me and gave Himself for me."
GALATIANS 2:20

Confess your trespasses to one another, and pray for one another, that you may be healed.
JAMES 5:16

Humble yourselves in the sight of the Lord, and He will lift you up.
JAMES 4:10

For I know that in me (that is, in my flesh) nothing good dwells; for to will is present with me, but how to perform what is good I do not find . . . I find then a law, that evil is present with me, the one who wills to do good. For I delight in the law of God according to the inward man.
ROMANS 7:18, 21–22

Right Thinking:

GOD IS WITH ME, I HAVE NOTHING TO FEAR.

Wrong Thinking:

I CAN'T SHAKE THESE FEELINGS OF WORRY AND FEAR.

Yea, though I walk through the valley of the shadow of death, I will fear no evil; for You are with me; Your rod and Your staff, they comfort me. You prepare a table before me in the presence of my enemies; You anoint my head with oil; my cup runs over.

PSALM 23:4–5

GOD IS WITH ME, I HAVE NOTHING TO FEAR

When you find yourself walking through valleys filled with shadows of fear and uncertainty, it's easy to feel as though you are walking alone in the darkness. But because God is with you, there is nothing to fear.

In Psalm 23:4–5, the scripture says, *Yea, though I walk through the valley of the shadow of death, I will fear no evil; for You are with me; Your rod and Your staff, they comfort me. You prepare a table before me in the presence of my enemies; You anoint my head with oil; my cup runs over.* This is a reminder of the comforting presence of God in the midst of life's trials. Even in your darkest moments, He is with you, guiding you with His rod and staff and providing for your needs abundantly.

When you choose to think thoughts of faith and trust in God's presence, it transforms your perspective on fear. Instead of allowing fear to paralyze you, boldly declare that God is with you and that He is greater than any obstacle you face. His presence brings comfort, peace, and assurance.

Matthew 18:19 says, *If two of you agree on earth . . . it will be done.* It's a reminder that when we stand in faith, lock arms with another believer, there's nothing that God won't do. But there's something else to consider: the same principle applies in the negative. When the Enemy tries to plant a seed of doubt or fear in your mind, he's extending an invitation for you to agree with him. And if you do, if you entertain those negative thoughts and give them your endorsement, you're essentially giving them the power to come to fruition in your life.

You have a choice. You have the power to reject those negative thoughts, to refuse to agree with the Enemy's lies. And when you do, you turn the tables. You take away his power and you instead align yourself with the truth of God's Word.

Instead of dwelling on feelings of worry and fear, fix your eyes on the One who is always by your side.

When you cultivate a relationship with God through prayer, worship, and meditation on His Word, you become more aware of His presence in your life. You begin to recognize His guiding hand and provision, even in the smallest details. And you recognize the lies of the Enemy for what they are.

Instead of dwelling on feelings of worry and fear, fix your eyes on the One who is always by your side. Get in agreement with His promises that say He'll never leave you nor forsake you, no matter what challenges come your way. As you surrender fear to Him and allow His peace to fill your heart, you can walk confidently in His presence, knowing that He is with you every step of the way.

If you're struggling with fear today, be mindful of what you're agreeing with. Reflect on God's faithfulness in the past and trust that He will continue to be faithful in the future. Take comfort in knowing that His presence is a shield of protection around you, and there is nothing to fear when He is with you.

Today, don't let the Enemy's lies take root. Instead, stand firm on the promises of God, and watch as He moves mountains on your behalf. May you experience His comfort, provision, and peace in abundance. And may you boldly declare, "Even though I walk through the valley of the shadow of death, I will fear no evil, for You are with me."

If you're struggling with fear today, be mindful of what you're agreeing with.

Power Up✛

"Fear not, for I am with you; be not dismayed, for I am your God. I will strengthen you, yes, I will help you, I will uphold you with My righteous right hand."
ISAIAH 41:10

Blessed be the God and Father of our Lord Jesus Christ, the Father of mercies and God of all comfort, who comforts us in all our tribulation, that we may be able to comfort those who are in any trouble, with the comfort with which we ourselves are comforted by God.
2 CORINTHIANS 1:3–4

The ransomed of the LORD shall return, and come to Zion with singing, with everlasting joy on their heads. They shall obtain joy and gladness; sorrow and sighing shall flee away.
ISAIAH 51:11

"This day is holy to our Lord. Do not sorrow, for the joy of the LORD is your strength."
NEHEMIAH 8:10

He spoke a parable to them, that men always ought to pray and not lose heart. . . .
LUKE 18:1

Right Thinking:

GOD IS GUIDING MY STEPS, OPENING DOORS OF OPPORTUNITY, LINING UP THE RIGHT CONNECTIONS.

Wrong Thinking:

I JUST DON'T KNOW WHAT TO DO.

I will instruct you and teach you in the way you should go; I will guide you with My eye.

PSALM 32:8

GOD IS GUIDING
MY STEPS

Do you feel like your path is one of uncertainty and indecision? Are you questioning your next move and feeling lost? Maybe you find yourself standing at a crossroads, unsure of which road to take or what decisions to make. If you feel overwhelmed and lost, you can trust that God is guiding your steps, opening doors of opportunity, and lining up the right connections.

Let me remind you of a fundamental truth about our God: He is not a God of randomness. He's not wish-washy or uncertain. No, our God is precise, exact. He has meticulously crafted the blueprint of your life down to the smallest detail.

The Bible assures us in Psalm 32:8, *I will instruct you and teach you in the way you should go; I will guide you with My eye.* These words are a powerful reminder that you are not alone in your journey. God, in His infinite wisdom and love, promises to lead and teach you the way you should go. He is intimately involved in every detail of your life, guiding with His gentle hand and watching over you with His loving eye.

When we choose to think thoughts of faith and trust in God's guidance, it changes our perspective on uncertainty. Instead of feeling overwhelmed by the unknown, we can rest assured that God is working behind the scenes, orchestrating events for our good. He is opening doors of opportunity that we may not even be aware of and lining up the right connections to help us along the way.

God's guidance isn't always loud or dramatic. Often, it comes in the form of gentle nudges, quiet whispers, or subtle signs. As you cultivate a listening ear and a heart sensitive to His leading, you can discern His voice amidst the noise of the world. You can trust that He will direct your steps with precision and clarity.

God's guidance isn't always loud or dramatic. Often, it comes in the form of gentle nudges, quiet whispers, or subtle signs.

Now, here's something that might surprise you: Just as God orchestrates good breaks and promotions and brings the right people into your life, He also strategically uses adversities, disappointments, and closed doors to propel you toward your destiny.

I've seen it firsthand. God doesn't always lead us down the most logical path. You might think you're going from point A to point B to point C in a straight line, but God's ways are far beyond our understanding. His roadmap resembles a series of stepping stones, with each stone strategically placed to lead you to your destination. You can trust Him even when you can't comprehend His plan. Your steps are strategically planned, for your good.

Instead of dwelling on feelings of confusion or indecision, fix your eyes on the One who holds your future in His hands. He knows the way you should go and will guide every step of the way.

If you're feeling unsure of what to do today, I want to encourage you to take a moment to seek God's guidance. Spend time in prayer, asking Him to lead you and teach you the way you should go. Open your heart to His direction and trust that He will make His will clear to you in His perfect timing.

Replace those thoughts of uncertainty with thoughts of faith and trust in God's guidance. Choose to believe that He is guiding your steps, opening doors of opportunity, and lining up the right connections for you. As you walk in obedience to His leading, may you experience His blessings and favor in abundance, and may you fulfill the purpose and destiny He has ordained for your life.

Spend time in prayer, asking Him to lead you and teach you the way you should go.

Power Up✝

Your ears shall hear a word behind you, saying, "This is the way, walk in it," whenever you turn to the right hand or whenever you turn to the left.
ISAIAH 30:21

If any of you lacks wisdom, let him ask of God, who gives to all liberally and without reproach, and it will be given to him. But let him ask in faith, with no doubting, for he who doubts is like a wave of the sea driven and tossed by the wind. For let not that man suppose that he will receive anything from the Lord; he is a double-minded man, unstable in all his ways.
JAMES 1:5–8

Cast your burden on the LORD, and He shall sustain you; He shall never permit the righteous to be moved.
PSALM 55:22

For God has not given us a spirit of fear, but of power and of love and of a sound mind.
2 TIMOTHY 1:7

Trust in the LORD with all your heart, and lean not on your own understanding; in all your ways acknowledge Him, and He shall direct your paths.
PROVERBS 3:5–6

Right Thinking:

GOD CAN HEAL MY HEART AND BRING ME OUT BETTER THAN BEFORE.

Wrong Thinking:

I DON'T SEE HOW I CAN EVER GET OVER THE PAIN OF THIS BROKEN RELATIONSHIP.

The LORD is near to those who have a broken heart, and saves such as have a contrite spirit.

PSALM 34:18

GOD CAN
HEAL MY HEART

I want to speak directly to your heart today. I know that life can sometimes throw unexpected curveballs, leaving you feeling broken and wounded by a relationship that didn't turn out the way you'd hoped. When you're feeling battered and bruised, it's easy to feel like you'll never recover, like the pain will never subside. But I want to remind you that God is near to the brokenhearted, and He is able to heal your heart and bring you out better than before.

The psalmist declares in Psalm 34:18, *The Lord is near to those who have a broken heart, and saves such as have a contrite spirit.* What a beautiful promise this is! God is not distant or aloof; He is close to you in your pain. He sees every tear you shed, and He longs to bring healing and restoration to your wounded heart.

You may feel like you're stuck in a cycle of despair, like your dreams are slipping away and that your heart will never mend. You may go through seasons of weeping, seasons of sorrow. It's not fair. But it's only a season. It's not permanent. You may think, *I don't see how my situation could ever work out with what I've been through, with what I'm up against. How could I ever be happy again?* God isn't going to leave you in a broken place, a wounded place, a lonely place. He is going to bring you out better. The suffering is a setup for God to show out in your life. He turns mourning into dancing, sorrow into joy.

Our God knows how to take an ugly scar, a painful divorce, an unexpected loss and turn it into something beautiful. One day you won't just think of the pain. You'll think of the goodness of God because He brought you through.

God is able to take our brokenness and turn it into something beautiful. He can mend the pieces of our shattered hearts and create a masterpiece of His grace and love. Cling to the promise that God is orchestrating a beautiful redemption story for your life.

God is near to the brokenhearted, and He is able to heal your heart and bring you out better than before.

I want you to know that you are not alone in your pain. God sees your hurt, and He cares deeply for you. He is not content to leave you in your brokenness; He desires to bring you out better than before. Surrender your pain to Him and allow Him to work in you and through you.

Healing is a process, and it may not happen overnight. But with God's strength, you can experience a deep and lasting healing that goes beyond what you could ever imagine. He is able to restore what was lost, redeem what was broken, and bring beauty from ashes.

If you're struggling to see how you could ever get over the pain of a broken relationship, turn to God. Spend time in prayer, pouring out your heart to Him and allowing Him to minister to you in your pain. Seek support from trusted friends and loved ones who can walk alongside you on your journey to healing. When you're heartbroken, remember that God feels it too. He's close to the brokenhearted, so He's right there with you in the midst of your pain. What was meant for your harm, He's going to turn for your good. Healing is coming. Freedom is coming.

Today, I declare over you that God can heal your heart and bring you out better than before. He is able to do exceedingly, abundantly above all that we ask or think. You are loved, cherished, and destined for greatness.

Seek support from trusted friends and loved ones who can walk alongside you on your journey to healing.

Power Up⁺

Blessed be the God and Father of our Lord Jesus Christ, the Father of mercies and God of all comfort, who comforts us in all our tribulation, that we may be able to comfort those who are in any trouble, with the comfort with which we ourselves are comforted by God.
2 CORINTHIANS 1:3–4

Sing, O heavens! Be joyful, O earth! And break out in singing, O mountains! For the LORD has comforted His people, and will have mercy on His afflicted.
ISAIAH 49:13

"When you pass through the waters, I will be with you; and through the rivers, they shall not overflow you. When you walk through the fire, you shall not be burned, nor shall the flame scorch you."
ISAIAH 43:2

Yea, though I walk through the valley of the shadow of death, I will fear no evil; for You are with me; Your rod and Your staff, they comfort me.
PSALM 23:4

"And God will wipe away every tear from their eyes; there shall be no more death, nor sorrow, nor crying. There shall be no more pain, for the former things have passed away."
REVELATION 21:4

Right Thinking:

I'M GOING TO DO WHAT IS RIGHT, REGARDLESS OF WHAT OTHERS DO OR HOW THEY TREAT ME.

Wrong Thinking:

NOBODY TREATS ME RIGHT. WHY SHOULD I TREAT OTHERS ANY BETTER?

And let us not grow weary while doing good, for in due season we shall reap if we do not lose heart.

GALATIANS 6:9

I'M GOING TO
DO WHAT IS RIGHT

I want to encourage you today that there is blessing in doing what is right, even when you don't see others treating you the way you want to be treated. In a world where negativity and mistreatment can often cloud our judgment, we have the power to choose righteousness, regardless of how others may treat us.

The Holy Spirit is your faithful guide. He will lead you to keep you on the best path. His voice may not boom loudly in your ears, but you'll hear His gentle whisper — a knowing, an impression upon your heart. Listen to that instruction. Don't brush it off.

God isn't asking you to obey for His own benefit. No, He's asking you to do it for your own sake, so He can elevate you and lead you into the fullness of your destiny.

The Bible tells us in Galatians 6:9, *And let us not grow weary while doing good, for in due season we shall reap if we do not lose heart.* Even when faced with challenges and opposition, we must not grow weary in doing what is right. For in due time, we will reap the rewards of our obedience if we do not lose heart.

Here's something I've learned: before God releases big blessings into your life, He often presents you with small tests. It could be as simple as showing kindness to a coworker who hasn't been kind to you, cleaning up a mess in the kitchen that you didn't make, or serving in the children's ministry without receiving any recognition. These might seem like inconveniences, but every time you obey, a blessing follows.

Instead of allowing yourself to be dragged down by negativity and bitterness, you can rise above the situation and respond with love, grace, and integrity. You can trust that God sees your actions and will honor them in His perfect timing.

The Holy Spirit is your faithful guide. He will lead you to keep you on the best path.

Choosing to do what is right is not always easy, especially when faced with injustice or mistreatment. But as believers, we are called to a higher standard. We are called to imitate Christ in all that we do, showing love and kindness to others even when it's difficult.

And here's the amazing part: God never asks you to do something without equipping you with the power to do it. Whatever tests you're facing right now, rest assured, you have the grace you need to overcome them.

God strategically places people in our paths so that we can be blessings to them. And every act of kindness, every seed of goodness you sow is planting a seed for God's blessing to be poured out upon you in abundance.

If you find yourself tempted to respond vengefully to those who mistreat you, I want to encourage you to take a moment to pause and reflect on the example of Jesus. He endured unimaginable suffering and mistreatment, yet He responded with love and forgiveness. He showed us that it is possible to overcome evil with good and that choosing righteousness ultimately leads to blessing and fulfillment.

Today, I want to challenge you to make a conscious decision to do what is right, regardless of how others may treat you. Be willing to step out, even if it means inconveniencing yourself. Choose to respond with love and kindness. Trust that God sees your actions and will honor them in His perfect timing. Follow His leading, and watch as He showers you with His blessings.

Be willing to step out, even if it means inconveniencing yourself.

Power Up✝

Let all bitterness, wrath, anger, clamor, and evil speaking be put away from you, with all malice. And be kind to one another, tenderhearted, forgiving one another, ever as God in Christ forgave you.
EPHESIANS 4:31–32

"Therefore, whatever you want men to do to you, do also to them, for this is the Law and the Prophets."
MATTHEW 7:12

Love suffers long and is kind; loves does not envy; love does not parade itself, is not puffed up; does not behave rudely, does not seek its own, is not provoked, thinks no evil; does not rejoice in iniquity, but rejoices in the truth; bears all things, believes all things, hopes all things, endures all things.
1 CORINTHIANS 13:4–7

He has shown you, O man, what is good; and what does the LORD require of you but to do justly, to love mercy, and to walk humbly with your God?
MICAH 6:8

So he answered and said, "'You shall love the LORD your God with all your heart, with all your soul, with all your strength, and with all your mind,' and 'your neighbor as yourself.'"
LUKE 10:27

Right Thinking:

GOD IS BRINGING THE RIGHT PEOPLE INTO MY LIFE.

Wrong Thinking:

I WILL NEVER FIND A TRUE FRIEND.

Two are better than one, because they have a good reward for their labor.

ECCLESIASTES 4:9

GOD IS BRINGING THE RIGHT PEOPLE INTO MY LIFE

I f you're feeling low on friends, declare today that God is bringing the right people into your life. It's easy to feel discouraged and lonely, especially when it seems like true friendship is hard to come by. But God has a divine plan for your relationships.

The Bible tells us in Ecclesiastes 4:9, *Two are better than one, because they have a good reward for their labor.* This verse highlights the importance of companionship and the blessing of having the right people by your side. God designed us for relationship, and He knows the desires of our hearts for meaningful connections with others.

You can rest assured that God is orchestrating divine connections that will enrich your life and bring you joy. There may be moments when you need borrowed faith from a friend. You may feel too discouraged, too weary, like you've been through too much to muster up faith on your own. And you know what? That's okay. God has a beautiful way of surrounding you with people who can carry faith on your behalf.

It could be someone who calls to let you know they're praying for you. It could be someone who stops by with an encouraging word when you need it most. It could even be a friend who lifts you up in prayer, interceding on your behalf and touching Heaven for you.

Trust in God's timing and provision for your relationships. Choose to believe that He is bringing the right people into your life at the right time. Instead of allowing feelings of doubt or discouragement to cloud your vision, choose to focus on the promise of God's faithfulness and pray for wisdom in how you can be a good friend.

Choose to believe that He is bringing the right people into your life at the right time.

Maybe you're in need of a friend with faith, someone to lean on when your own faith feels shaky. God can bring you those people. Or perhaps you're reading this today because God wants to remind you to be that friend with faith for someone else. Yes, you have the power to not only believe for yourself but also to let someone else borrow your faith in their time of need.

So, reach out to that discouraged coworker, visit that neighbor who's mourning loss, or encourage that relative who's lost their zeal and given up on their dreams. God is counting on you to be a beacon of hope to others as well.

As you go out each day, remember to represent God by standing in faith with someone, being an encouragement, lifting others up. Be a shining witness of His love and mercy. When you shine brightly, you'll attract favor with others and see situations turn around.

God's timing is perfect, and He knows exactly what you need and when you need it. He sees the desires of your heart and delights in giving good gifts. Surrender your relationships to Him and trust in His guidance. He will lead you to the right people who will uplift, encourage, and support you on your journey. In return, you can be that one to uplift, encourage, and support others.

Take a moment to pray and ask God to bring the right people into your life. Ask Him to show you when someone else might need to borrow faith. And in the meantime, focus on being the kind of friend that you desire to have, extending love, kindness, and grace to those around you.

God's timing is perfect, and He knows exactly what you need and when you need it.

Power Up⁺

A friend loves at all times, and a brother is born for adversity.

PROVERBS 17:17

For as the body is one and has many members, but all the members of that one body, being many, are one body, so also is Christ.

1 CORINTHIANS 12:12

Let brotherly love continue. Do not forget to entertain strangers, for by so doing some have unwittingly entertained angels.

HEBREWS 13:1–2

Everyone helped his neighbor, and said to his brother, "Be of good courage!"

ISAIAH 41:6

"For whoever does the will of My Father in heaven is My brother and sister and mother."

MATTHEW 12:50

Let all that you do be done with love.

1 CORINTHIANS 16:14

For you, brethren, have been called to liberty; only do not use liberty as an opportunity for the flesh, but through love serve one another.

GALATIANS 5:13

Right Thinking:

I REFUSE TO BE HELD BACK BY BITTERNESS AND UNFORGIVENESS. INSTEAD, I CHOOSE TO FORGIVE AND RECEIVE GOD'S HEALING FOR MY SOUL.

Wrong Thinking:

I CAN NEVER FORGIVE WHAT WAS DONE TO ME.

Let all bitterness, wrath, anger, clamor, and evil speaking be put away from you, with all malice. And be kind to one another, tenderhearted, forgiving one another, even as God in Christ forgave you.

EPHESIANS 4:31–32

I REFUSE TO BE HELD BACK BY BITTERNESS

There is a transformative power in forgiveness and the healing that it brings to our souls. It's easy to hold onto bitterness and unforgiveness, especially when we've been hurt deeply, but I want to encourage you to make up your mind to choose forgiveness instead.

Holding onto bitterness and unforgiveness only weighs you down and keeps you trapped in the past. It robs you of your joy and peace and prevents you from experiencing the fullness of God's blessings in your life. But when you choose to forgive, you open the door to healing and restoration for your soul.

The Bible tells us in Ephesians 4:31–32, *Let all bitterness, wrath, anger, clamor, and evil speaking be put away from you, with all malice. And be kind to one another, tenderhearted, forgiving one another, even as God in Christ forgave you.* These words are a powerful reminder of the importance of forgiveness in our lives.

Instead of allowing ourselves to be consumed by anger and resentment, we can choose to extend grace and mercy to those who have wronged us. We can trust in God's promise to heal our hearts and restore our souls as we forgive others, just as He has forgiven us through Christ.

Choose to release the weight of resentment and anger that you've been carrying and allow God's healing to flow into your soul. Instead of holding onto grudges, extend grace and kindness to others, just as God has done for you. Trust in God's ability to bring beauty from ashes. As we choose to forgive, we open ourselves up to the healing power of God's love and grace.

We all face moments of hurt and betrayal, but you have a choice in how you respond. You can cling to the pain, allowing bitterness and anger to fester inside and poison your future. Or you can choose to forgive and trust in the Almighty to redeem what was lost.

Holding onto bitterness and unforgiveness only weighs you down and keeps you trapped in the past.

You may think that the wounds are too deep, that forgiveness is beyond your reach. But let me assure you: it is not about excusing things that were done to you; it's about freeing yourself from the chains of resentment and bitterness. When you forgive, you take away the power that those who hurt you have held over your life.

Forgiveness is a journey, and it's okay if you don't feel capable of forgiveness in this moment. You can cultivate the desire to forgive and ask God to help you each day. As you seek His help, those negative emotions will gradually fade until one day you realize they hold no power over you at all.

So, take heart and embark on the journey of forgiveness. Release the burdens of the past and embrace the freedom that forgiveness brings. In letting it go, you are paving the way for a future filled with joy, peace, and hope.

Release the burdens of the past and embrace the freedom that forgiveness brings.

Power Up✝

"But if you do not forgive men their trespasses, neither will your Father forgive your trespasses."
MATTHEW 6:15

. . . bearing with one another, and forgiving one another, if anyone has a complaint against another; even as Christ forgave you, so you also must do.
COLOSSIANS 3:13

Now may the God of patience and comfort grant you to be like-minded toward one another, according to Christ Jesus, that you may with one mind and one mouth glorify the God and Father of our Lord Jesus Christ. Therefore receive one another, just as Christ also received us, to the glory of God.
ROMANS 15:5–7

. . . not returning evil for evil or reviling for reviling, but on the contrary blessing, knowing that you were called to this, that you may inherit a blessing.
1 PETER 3:9

"And forgive us our sins, for we also forgive everyone who is indebted to us."
LUKE 11:4

I CHOOSE TO LIVE MY LIFE HAPPY AND BLOOM WHERE I'M PLANTED. THE JOY OF THE LORD IS MY STRENGTH.

Wrong Thinking:

I DON'T FEEL LIKE I'M EVER GOING TO BE HAPPY.

You have put gladness in my heart, more than in the season that their grain and wine increased.

PSALM 4:7

I CHOOSE TO LIVE MY LIFE HAPPY

When we wake up each morning, we have the incredible privilege of choosing how we're going to live that day. We can choose to live in faith, with hearts full of joy, expecting favor at every turn. Or we can choose to live in a state of discouragement, feeling defeated and allowing our problems to consume us.

Maybe today you feel overwhelmed by challenges and uncertainties, like you're never going to be happy again. But happiness is a choice. No matter the circumstances, you can live with joy and bloom where you're planted.

The Bible says in Psalm 4:7, *You have put gladness in my heart, more than in the season that their grain and wine increased.* Our joy comes from the Lord Himself. It's not dependent on external circumstances or the ups and downs of life; it flows from the deep well of His love and presence within.

Now, here's the thing about happiness: it doesn't just happen to us. It's a conscious decision that we must make each and every day. You can't wait around to see what kind of day it's going to be; you have to decide what kind of day it's going to be. Right from the moment you open your eyes in the morning, it's time to make up your mind and choose happiness.

When you choose to think thoughts of happiness and joy, it changes your perspective on life. Instead of allowing yourself to be consumed by negativity or despair, you can embrace each day as a gift from God and find reasons to rejoice in the midst of challenges. You can trust that God is working all things together for your good and that His joy gives you the strength to overcome any obstacle.

Decide right now that you will not allow your circumstances to dictate your happiness and that you will find reasons to rejoice in every situation. Instead of focusing on what's wrong or missing, focus on what's right and present. Look for the blessings that surround you, both big and small, and give God thanks for them.

Right from the moment you open your eyes in the morning, it's time to make up your mind and choose happiness.

You and I are not here by accident. God handpicked you to be alive in this moment, to wake up this morning, to have strength to rise from your bed. He has crowned you with favor, planted seeds of greatness within you, and declared you to be more than a conqueror, the head and not the tail. And one of the ways we honor God is by living joyfully.

As you choose joy in your life, you will find that it becomes a natural part of who you are. You will bloom where you're planted, spreading happiness to those around you. As people of faith, we have a source of strength that goes beyond our own abilities. The joy of the Lord is our strength, and it empowers us to live victoriously.

So, don't waste another moment being negative, discouraged, focused on what didn't work out. Reclaim your joy. Live each day in faith. Make the most of it and embrace the gift of today with a heart full of gratitude and joy. And as you embrace the joy of the Lord as your strength, you will discover that there is no obstacle too great for you to overcome.

As you choose joy in your life, you will find that it becomes a natural part of who you are.

Power Up✝

For God gives wisdom and knowledge and joy to a man who is good in His sight; but to the sinner He gives the work of gathering and collecting, that he may give to him who is good before God. This also is vanity and grasping for the wind.
ECCLESIASTES 2:26

Finally, my brethren, rejoice in the Lord. For me to write the same things to you is not tedious, but for you it is safe.
PHILIPPIANS 3:1

And they worshiped Him, and returned to Jerusalem with great joy. . . .
LUKE 24:52

And not only that, but we also rejoice in God through our Lord Jesus Christ, through whom we have now received the reconciliation.
ROMANS 5:11

Your words were found, and I ate them, and Your word was to me the joy and rejoicing of my heart; for I am called by Your name, O LORD God of hosts.
JEREMIAH 15:16

Right Thinking:

THERE IS AN ANOINTING OF EASE ON MY LIFE. GOD IS GOING BEFORE ME TO MAKE THE CROOKED PLACES STRAIGHT.

Wrong Thinking:

I'M SO TIRED; NOTHING I DO EVER SEEMS TO WORK.

I would have lost heart, unless I had believed that I would see the goodness of the LORD in the land of the living. Wait on the LORD; be of good courage, and He shall strengthen your heart; wait, I say, on the LORD!

PSALM 27:13–14

THERE IS AN ANOINTING OF EASE ON MY LIFE

I f you're tired and weary today, let me remind you that there is an anointing of ease on your life. God is going before you to make the crooked places straight. He has a plan and a purpose for your life, and He will lead you into a place of ease and abundance.

Scripture tells us in Psalm 27:13–14, *I would have lost heart, unless I had believed that I would see the goodness of the LORD in the land of the living. Wait on the LORD; be of good courage, and He shall strengthen your heart; wait, I say, on the LORD!* Even when things seem difficult or uncertain, you can have confidence that God is working to bring about His perfect plan.

You can rest assured that God is working all things together for your good. He is going before you, smoothing out the rough patches and opening doors of opportunity that you could never have imagined.

In Matthew 11:30, Jesus tells us, *"My yoke is easy and My burden is light."* This is a promise to cling to. It's a reminder that, yes, we will face times of struggle, but these trials are not permanent. What the Lord places upon us, His yoke, is not heavy or burdensome — it's easy, it's light.

You may be in the midst of a struggle right now. You may feel a weight bearing down on you, believing that this is just how it's always going to be — struggling in your health, your finances, your relationships. But let me tell you: get ready, because you're going to step into an anointing of ease.

What once felt like an insurmountable struggle will no longer weigh you down. There will be a supernatural grace, a divine favor that lightens your load and takes the pressure off. God has promised to go before you, making your crooked paths straight and smoothing out the rough patches.

God is going before you to make the crooked places straight.

Choose to believe that there is an anointing of ease on your life and that God is leading you into a season of abundance and blessing. Focus on the promises of God and the incredible future He has in store for you.

Take heart. You're entering a season where things will fall into place. Unexpected breakthroughs are on the horizon, and problems that seemed insurmountable are about to turn around. You're not meant to go through life constantly struggling, pressured, or weighed down. This is a new day — a day of ease and favor.

If you find yourself feeling tired or discouraged, take a moment to pause and reflect on the goodness of God. Think about all the ways He has provided for you and the times He has come through for you in the past.

As you continue to wait on the Lord, you will begin to see His anointing of ease manifest in your life. Doors will open, obstacles will be removed, and you will step into a season of abundance and blessing like never before. So, lift your head high, embrace this promise, and step forward in faith, knowing that ease is on its way. Trust in God's timing and watch as He orchestrates miracles that will leave you in awe. Ease is coming. Receive it.

Trust in God's timing and watch as He orchestrates miracles that will leave you in awe.

Power Up✝

Be of good courage, and He shall strengthen your heart, all you who hope in the LORD.
PSALM 31:24

We are hard-pressed on every side, yet not crushed; we are perplexed, but not in despair; persecuted, but not forsaken; struck down, but not destroyed. . . .
2 CORINTHIANS 4:8–9

. . . being confident of this very thing, that He who has begun a good work in you will complete it until the day of Jesus Christ.
PHILIPPIANS 1:6

"Peace I leave with you, My peace I give to you; not as the world gives do I give to you. Let not your heart be troubled, neither let it be afraid."
JOHN 14:27

Though I walk in the midst of trouble, You will revive me; You will stretch out Your hand against the wrath of my enemies, and Your right hand will save me.
PSALM 138:7

I AM THE VERY RIGHTEOUSNESS OF GOD IN CHRIST JESUS. I CAN COME BOLDLY BEFORE HIS THRONE OF GRACE.

Wrong Thinking:

I FEEL SO MUCH SHAME OVER THE MISTAKES I'VE MADE.

MY EMOTIONS

He has not dealt with us according to our sins, nor punished us according to our iniquities. For as the heavens are high above the earth, so great is His mercy toward those who fear Him; as far as the east is from the west, so far has He removed our transgressions from us.

PSALM 103:10–12

I AM THE VERY RIGHTEOUSNESS OF GOD IN CHRIST JESUS

I want to remind you today of the incredible truth of who you are in Christ Jesus. When you allow feelings of shame and condemnation to weigh you down, focusing on your past mistakes and shortcomings, you end up feeling guilty and unworthy, as if you don't deserve God's goodness. We often use shame as a tool to try and motivate ourselves or others to do better, but the truth is shame has the opposite effect.

I want to encourage you to shift your perspective and embrace the righteousness that is yours through Jesus Christ. Romans 8:1 says, *There is therefore now no condemnation to those who are in Christ Jesus, who do not walk according to the flesh, but according to the Spirit.* Read that again and soak in the freedom we have in Christ. When you come to Him in repentance and faith, He washes away your sins and clothes you with His righteousness. There is no condemnation for those who are in Him — only love, mercy, and grace.

Psalm 103:10–12 reminds us of the boundless mercy and forgiveness of our God. It says, *He has not dealt with us according to our sins, nor punished us according to our iniquities. For as the heavens are high above the earth, so great is His mercy toward those who fear Him; as far as the east is from the west, so far has He removed our transgressions from us.* What a comfort this is! God's mercy is limitless, and His forgiveness knows no bounds. He removes your sins from as far as the east is from the west, never to be remembered again.

Even the heroes of faith had their moments of weakness. Just look at Peter — one day preaching to thousands, the next cursing and denying Jesus. And David, a man after God's own heart, found himself committing adultery and murder. Noah, who built the ark and saved his family, also had his moments of weakness. Yet despite their failures, they found restoration when they confessed their faults and turned to God.

There is no condemnation for those who are in Him — only love, mercy, and grace.

Let me remind you: God has made you righteous. Yes, righteous — blameless, honorable, holy. And here's the kicker: you are righteous right now, not because of anything you've done but because of what Christ has done for you. You can't earn righteousness through your own efforts; it's a gift freely given to all who receive it.

Shame and condemnation don't define you, so you can boldly approach the throne of grace with confidence, knowing that you are loved and accepted by your Heavenly Father. You can trust that His mercy is greater than your failures, and His grace is sufficient to cover all of your sins.

If you see yourself as unworthy, undeserving, and constantly falling short, you're probably not fully embracing the gift of righteousness. The accuser may whisper lies, reminding you of your failures and mistakes, but God declares you to be holy, blameless, and anointed.

Who will you believe today? Will you continue to carry the weight of guilt and shame, or will you start receiving the gift of righteousness that God offers you? Embrace your identity as the righteousness of God in Christ Jesus. Choose to believe that you are forgiven, loved, and accepted by God just as you are. Instead of dwelling on your past mistakes, focus on the amazing grace that has been lavished upon you through Jesus Christ. Allow His love to wash over you and fill you with peace and joy. Choose to walk in the freedom that is yours.

Choose to believe that you are forgiven, loved, and accepted by God just as you are.

Power Up✛

There is therefore now no condemnation to those who are in Christ Jesus, who do not walk according to the flesh, but according to the Spirit.
ROMANS 8:1

Blessed is he whose transgression is forgiven, whose sin is covered.
PSALM 32:1

"For if you return to the LORD, your brethren and your children will be treated with compassion by those who lead them captive, so that they may come back to this land; for the LORD your God is gracious and merciful, and will not turn His face from you if you return to Him."
2 CHRONICLES 30:9

"No more shall every man teach his neighbor, and every man his brother, saying, 'Know the LORD,' for they all shall know Me, from the least of them to the greatest of them, says the LORD. For I will forgive their iniquity, and their sin I will remember no more."
JEREMIAH 31:34

Let the wicked forsake his way, and the unrighteous man his thoughts; let him return to the LORD, and He will have mercy on him; and to our God, for He will abundantly pardon.
ISAIAH 55:7

GOD CAN DO A "SUDDENLY" MIRACLE IN MY LIFE. HIS TIMING IS PERFECT. I TRUST HIM.

Wrong Thinking:

I'VE BEEN SICK FOR SO LONG; IT WILL NEVER END.

This I recall to my mind, therefore I have hope. Through the LORD's mercies we are not consumed, because His compassions fail not. They are new every morning; great is Your faithfulness. "The LORD is my portion," says my soul, "Therefore I hope in Him!" The LORD is good to those who wait for Him, to the soul who seeks Him. It is good that one should hope and wait quietly for the salvation of the LORD.

LAMENTATIONS 3:21–26

GOD CAN DO A "SUDDENLY" MIRACLE IN MY LIFE

Today I want to encourage you to believe in God's ability to perform "suddenly" miracles in your life. You may have been patiently waiting, diligently praying, and believing for change, yet haven't seen any improvement. You feel discouraged and have resigned yourself to the idea that things will remain the same for a long time, that you simply have to endure it. It's especially disheartening when you're facing long-standing challenges or illnesses, but I want to encourage you to shift your perspective and believe for a "suddenly" miracle in your life.

In Isaiah 60:22, God declares, *"I am the LORD, and when it is time, I will make these things happen quickly"* (NCV). There are certain moments in your life that God has ordained for a quick work — a sudden turnaround that happens much faster than you ever imagined. Even if it seems like nothing is changing, even if you feel no closer to your breakthrough than you did last year, when your time comes, God will move swiftly.

The Bible tells us in Lamentations 3:21–26, *This I recall to my mind, therefore I have hope. Through the LORD's mercies we are not consumed, because His compassions fail not. They are new every morning; great is Your faithfulness. "The LORD is my portion," says my soul, "Therefore I hope in Him!" The LORD is good to those who wait for Him, to the soul who seeks Him. It is good that one should hope and wait quietly for the salvation of the LORD.*

When you remind yourself of God's ability to perform "suddenly" miracles, it changes your perspective on your circumstances. You can rest assured that God is working. His mercies are new every morning, and His compassion toward us never fails.

If you're facing a health issue, get ready, because God can move in an unusual, out-of-the-ordinary way. And when He does, you'll know it's the hand of God orchestrating your rapid recovery, your sudden breakthrough.

> **His mercies are new every morning, and His compassion toward us never fails.**

Don't lose hope. Keep believing, keep trusting, for your healing is closer than you think. Choose to believe that He can perform a "suddenly" miracle in your situation, no matter how long you've been struggling. Instead of focusing on the length of time you've been sick or facing challenges, focus on the greatness of God who is able to do exceedingly, abundantly above all that you ask or think.

If you find yourself feeling discouraged or hopeless, take a moment to meditate on the goodness of God. Spend time reading scriptures of the miraculous to boost your faith. Remember His faithfulness in the past and the times He has come through for you in miraculous ways. Choose to trust in His promises and believe that He can do a "suddenly" miracle in your life.

As you continue to trust in God's perfect timing and believe in His ability to perform miracles, you will see His hand at work in your life. Healing will come and breakthroughs will happen in ways you never thought possible. Trust His timing and see the "suddenly" happen.

Spend time reading scriptures of the miraculous to boost your faith.

Power Up⁺

I would have lost heart, unless I had believed that I would see the goodness of the LORD in the land of the living. Wait on the LORD; be of good courage, and He shall strengthen your heart; wait, I say, on the LORD!
PSALM 27:13–14

Lead me in Your truth and teach me, for You are the God of my salvation; on You I wait all the day.
PSALM 25:5

*I wait for the LORD, my soul waits,
and in His word I do hope.*
PSALM 130:5

Indeed, let no one who waits on You be ashamed; let those be ashamed who deal treacherously without cause. Show me Your ways, O LORD; teach me Your paths.
PSALM 25:3–4

The eyes of all look expectantly to You, and You give them their food in due season. You open Your hand and satisfy the desire of every living thing.
PSALM 145:15–16

14

NO MATTER HOW I FEEL, I WILL PRAISE GOD AND DECLARE HIS FAITHFULNESS OVER MYSELF AND MY LOVED ONES.

Wrong Thinking:

I FIND MYSELF COMPLAINING ALL THE TIME BECAUSE OF MY SICKNESS.

Therefore by Him let us continually offer the sacrifice of praise to God, that is, the fruit of our lips, giving thanks to His name.

HEBREWS 13:15

MY HEALTH

NO MATTER HOW I FEEL, I WILL PRAISE GOD

When sickness has been part of your life for an extended time, you can easily default to complaining, feeling sorry for yourself, feeling discouraged. But no matter where you find yourself, in both the health of your mind and your body, you can choose to praise. You can declare God's faithfulness over yourself and your loved ones.

Scripture tells us in Hebrews 13:15, *Therefore by Him let us continually offer the sacrifice of praise to God, that is, the fruit of our lips, giving thanks to His name.* Even in the midst of sickness or trials, we can choose to lift our voices in praise and thanksgiving for His faithfulness and goodness.

God wants to remind you today that everything is going to work out. He is in complete control. He sees the medical report. He knows the challenges you're facing. And He wants to reassure you: He will not fail you. He will not let you down. That problem, that sickness, that situation is not going to overcome you.

Praise and thanksgiving does something for us. It shifts our focus from our circumstances to the ultimate Healer, the God who keeps His Word. Instead of dwelling on the situation or pleading with God to help you, choose to remember His Word.

Take hold of His promises and remind yourself of what He has said. Say, "God, You promised to be close to the brokenhearted. I'm hurting, but You promised to give me beauty for ashes. You said that while we may endure weeping for a night, joy comes in the morning." These are promises that God is bound to fulfill. And when I say "bound," I'm not suggesting that we're commanding God or dictating His actions. No, it's a principle; God is faithful to His Word. It's against His very nature to deceive or break His Word.

I want to challenge you today to praise God and declare His faithfulness. Praise is not dependent on our feelings. His promises are true no matter how you feel. God is faithful. You can trust in Him.

Say, "God, I trust that You will never fail me or let me down. Even though this situation seems like a disappointment, I believe that all things are working together for my good. It may not look good right now, but I am confident that one day I will look back and see how You used this for my benefit in the grand plan of my life."

Faith is about trust. It's about knowing, deep within your soul, that God has your best interests at heart. So, hold on to that trust, cling to His promises, and watch as He moves mightily on your behalf.

> Take hold of His promises and remind yourself of what He has said.

As you continue to choose praise over complaint and declare God's faithfulness in every situation, you will begin to see His hand at work in your life in amazing ways. His peace will fill your heart, His joy will be your strength, and His presence will surround you like a shield. So, let us choose to think thoughts of praise and thanksgiving, knowing that our God is faithful and worthy of all our praise.

Let us choose to think thoughts of praise and thanksgiving.

Power Up⁺

And when he had consulted with the people, he appointed those who should sing to the LORD, and who should praise the beauty of holiness, as they went out before the army and were saying: "Praise the LORD, for His mercy endures forever."
2 CHRONICLES 20:21

"Worthy is the Lamb who was slain to receive power and riches and wisdom, and strength and honor and glory and blessing!"
REVELATION 5:12

You who fear the LORD, praise Him! All you descendants of Jacob, glorify Him, and fear Him, all you offspring of Israel!
PSALM 22:23

Oh, that men would give thanks to the LORD for His goodness, and for His wonderful works to the children of men!
PSALM 107:8

Daniel answered and said: "Blessed be the name of God forever and ever, for wisdom and might are His."
DANIEL 2:20

15

Right Thinking:

I AM A CHILD OF ALMIGHTY GOD WITH ROYAL DNA RUNNING THROUGH MY VEINS. HE IS A PERFECT FATHER WHO LOVES ME UNCONDITIONALLY.

Wrong Thinking:

I DON'T SEE HOW GOD COULD LOVE ME.

But God, who is rich in mercy, because of His great love with which He loved us, even when we were dead in trespasses, made us alive together with Christ (by grace you have been saved), and raised us up together, and made us sit together in the heavenly places in Christ Jesus, that in the ages to come He might show the exceeding riches of His grace in His kindness toward us in Christ Jesus.

EPHESIANS 2:4–7

MY HEALTH

I AM A CHILD
OF ALMIGHTY GOD

Let me remind you of your identity as a beloved child of Almighty God. You likely hold a deep reverence and awe for God, and that's commendable. But don't forget this truth: amidst His majesty as the King of Kings, the awesome Creator, He is also your Heavenly Father.

He longs to hear from you. That's why when Jesus taught us how to pray with the Lord's Prayer, He didn't say to begin with titles like "King of Kings" or "Holy Creator of the Universe," though those titles are certainly fitting to describe the Lord. But Jesus emphasized we should address God as *"Our Father which art in heaven"* (Matthew 6:9, KJV). Jesus wanted us to perceive God not only as all-powerful and majestic — which He is — but also as a loving Father. He is someone intimately close to us, who listens and guides us through life's journey.

As a child of God, you are fearfully and wonderfully made, with royal DNA running through your veins. You are a cherished child of the Most High, and His love for you knows no bounds.

Think about this for a moment: You are not just a random creation wandering aimlessly through life. No, you are a masterpiece crafted by the hands of a loving Father who has a perfect plan and purpose for your life. He has endowed you with royal DNA, with all the qualities and characteristics of His divine nature. You are His beloved and He delights in you.

Ephesians 2:4–7 says, *But God, who is rich in mercy, because of His great love with which He loved us, even when we were dead in trespasses, made us alive together with Christ (by grace you have been saved), and raised us up together, and made us sit together in the heavenly places in Christ Jesus, that in the ages to come He might show the exceeding riches of His grace in His kindness toward us in Christ Jesus.* You may not be able to see how God could love you, but the truth is that He loves you so much that He went to great lengths to show the riches of His grace toward you.

As a child of God, you are fearfully and wonderfully made, with royal DNA running through your veins.

Embracing your identity as a child of God changes your perspective of yourself and your relationship with Him. You can trust in His perfect love to guide you, protect you, and empower you to fulfill your divine destiny.

If your earthly father wasn't the best role model, don't let that tarnish your perception of your Heavenly Father. He is merciful, forgiving, and overflowing with love for you. He takes great pride in you and delights in showcasing you to the world. He sees the potential within you and believes in your greatness.

Remember, you don't need an intermediary to speak to God. You have a direct line to your Heavenly Father, and He is always ready to listen. When you start seeing God as a loving Father, you no longer have to live under the weight of guilt or condemnation. You can walk in strength, confidence, and security.

God's love for you is not based on anything you have done or will ever do. It is based solely on who He is as a perfect Father. He sees you as precious and valuable, and He delights in showering His love upon you each and every day.

I declare over you today that as you embrace the image of God as your Father, you will step into everything He has destined you to be. You will walk in the knowledge that you are deeply loved and cherished by your Heavenly Father, and nothing can ever separate you from His love. You are loved unconditionally — now and for all eternity.

When you start seeing God as a loving Father, you no longer have to live under the weight of guilt or condemnation.

Power Up⁺

"Yes, I have loved you with an everlasting love; therefore with lovingkindness I have drawn you."
JEREMIAH 31:3

In this is love, not that we loved God, but that He loved us and sent His Son to be the propitiation for our sins. Beloved, if God so loved us, we also ought to love one another.
1 JOHN 4:10–11

For I am persuaded that neither death nor life, nor angels nor principalities nor powers, nor things present nor things to come, nor height nor depth, nor any other created thing, shall be able to separate us from the love of God which is in Christ Jesus our Lord.
ROMANS 8:38–39

"As the Father loved Me, I also have loved you; abide in My love. If you keep My commandments, you will abide in My love, just as I have kept My Father's commandments and abide in His love."
JOHN 15:9–10

Beloved, let us love one another, for love is of God; and everyone who loves is born of God and knows God. He who does not love does not know God, for God is love.
1 JOHN 4:7–8

Right Thinking:

I SUBMIT MY LIFE TO GOD'S WORD AND HIS PURPOSES FOR ME.

Wrong Thinking:

I WANT TO MAKE MY DECISIONS AND DO THINGS MY OWN WAY.

"Blessed is the man who trusts in the LORD, and whose hope is the LORD."

JEREMIAH 17:7

MY HEALTH

I SUBMIT MY LIFE
TO GOD'S WORD

As humans, our default is to want to do things our own way. Submitting does not sound like freedom, but I want to encourage you today that submitting your life to God's Word and purposes will bring you greater freedom than you thought possible. When you trust in the Lord, submitting your life to His purposes, you'll have supernatural direction. You can lean on your trust in the wisdom and guidance of our Heavenly Father.

As it says in Proverbs 3:5–6, *Trust in the LORD with all your heart, and lean not on your own understanding; in all your ways acknowledge Him, and He shall direct your paths.* You can lean on your own understanding and have plans that match your human limitations. Or you can lean on God, trusting that His ways are higher, and let Him supernaturally direct your life.

When you trust in the wisdom and guidance of your Heavenly Father, you can rest assured that He knows what is best for you and will direct your paths in accordance with His perfect plan. Living submitted may sound challenging, but remember: when God presents you with a challenge, He also provides the grace you need to overcome it. Step into that grace.

The older I get, the more I find myself praying, "God, not my will, but Your will be done." I've learned to stop fighting against closed doors and to stop becoming frustrated when things don't unfold as quickly as I'd like. I know that God is always in control. As long as you're honoring Him, you can rest assured that in due time God will lead you where you need to be.

Even when it may not align with your own plans or desires, you can trust that God's plan is better than anything you could dream up. Instead of trying to figure everything out on your own, acknowledge God in all your ways and allow Him to direct your paths.

When God presents you with a challenge, He also provides the grace you need to overcome it.

God's ways are higher than our ways, and His thoughts are higher than our thoughts. He sees the bigger picture and knows what is best for us in every situation. As you surrender to His will and trust in His guidance, He will lead you down the paths of righteousness and blessing.

While I wholeheartedly believe in praying for your dreams and expecting great things, I've also learned the importance of surrendering to God's timing and methods. Hold tightly to His promises and the desires He's placed within your heart, but remain flexible in how those dreams unfold. Don't become disheartened if things don't transpire exactly as you anticipated. Remember, God is always at work, orchestrating His perfect plan for your life. So, keep trusting and believing, and watch as He leads you into greater blessings than you ever thought possible.

As you continue to surrender to God's Word and His purposes for your life, you will experience a new-found sense of peace, joy, and fulfillment. You will walk in alignment with His will and experience His blessings in abundance. So, choose submission and trust in God's perfect plan, knowing that He will direct your paths and lead you into His abundant life.

God is always at work, orchestrating His perfect plan for your life.

Power Up⁺

Commit your works to the LORD, and your thoughts will be established.
PROVERBS 16:3

"If you are willing and obedient, you shall eat the good of the land; but if you refuse and rebel, you shall be devoured by the sword"; for the mouth of the LORD has spoken.
ISAIAH 1:19–20

Let this mind be in you which was also in Christ Jesus, who, being in the form of God, did not consider it robbery to be equal with God, but made Himself of no reputation, taking the form of a bondservant, and coming in the likeness of men. And being found in appearance as a man, He humbled Himself and became obedient to the point of death, even the death of the cross.
PHILIPPIANS 2:5–8

Therefore gird up the loins of your mind, be sober, and rest your hope fully upon the grace that is to be brought to you at the revelation of Jesus Christ; as obedient children, not conforming yourselves to the former lusts, as in your ignorance. . . .
1 PETER 1:13–14

17

NOT ONLY DOES GOD HEAR MY PRAYER, BUT HE IS ALREADY MAKING A WAY FOR ME. I MAY NOT SEE IT YET, BUT I'M GOING TO STAY IN FAITH, TRUSTING HIS PROMISES.

Wrong Thinking:

I PRAY AND PRAY, BUT GOD DOESN'T SEEM TO HEAR.

The LORD is near to all who call upon Him, to all who call upon Him in truth. He will fulfill the desire of those who fear Him; He also will hear their cry and save them.

PSALM 145:18–19

MY HEALTH

HE IS ALREADY MAKING
A WAY FOR ME

Do you ever feel like your prayers aren't getting through, like God is either not hearing you or not responding? Today's encouragement is to stay in faith, holding onto the unwavering belief that God can make a way for you, even when you cannot see it with your own eyes. When we don't see immediate results from our prayers, we naturally get discouraged, but I want to encourage you to shift your perspective and trust in the promises of our faithful God.

Think about it for a moment: not only does God hear your prayers, but He is already at work behind the scenes, orchestrating events and making a way for you. You may not see it yet, but you can stay in faith, knowing that He who promised is faithful to fulfill His Word.

The Bible tells us in Psalm 145:18–19, *The LORD is near to all who call upon Him, to all who call upon Him in truth. He will fulfill the desire of those who fear Him; He also will hear their cry and save them.* He is both near and faithful to His children. He hears the cries of His children and will save them. He listens and responds in action.

This is a thought I frequently find comfort in: *nothing catches God by surprise.* Every challenge, every obstacle, every trial that comes your way is already known to Him. The Enemy may try to whisper lies of defeat, but let me declare to you right now: The Enemy does not have the final say! God, he Almighty, holds the final say in your life.

In His Word, He assures us that we are more than conquerors through Him who loves us. He promises to always lead us in triumph. So, when fear comes knocking at your door, threatening to overwhelm you with doubt and despair, remember this: fear has no place in the heart of a believer!

Every challenge, every obstacle, every trial that comes your way is already known to Him.

Instead of entertaining fearful or hopeless thoughts, choose to answer the door of your heart with faith. Speak out loud the promises of God! Declare with boldness, "God, You said that You will fulfill the number of my days. You said Your plans for me are for good and not for evil. You said that what the Enemy meant for harm, You will turn around for my advantage. You said that when the Enemy comes in like a flood, Your favor will pour out!"

I want to challenge you today to make a conscious decision to stay in faith and trust in God's promises, even when you don't see immediate results from your prayers. Choose to believe that He hears your cry and is already at work on your behalf. Instead of focusing on what you cannot see, focus on the truth of God's Word and the assurance of His faithfulness.

If you find yourself struggling with doubt or impatience in your prayer life, think about all the times He has answered your prayers and come through for you in miraculous ways. As you continue to trust in God's promises, you will experience His peace that surpasses all understanding. You will walk in the fullness of His blessings and provision.

Let faith rise up within you like a mighty warrior, standing firm against the onslaught of fear. For our God is with us; His strength is our refuge; and His promises are our shield. Next time doubt or fear knock, let faith get the door!

Choose to believe that He hears your cry and is already at work on your behalf.

Power Up✝

"And whatever you ask in My name, that I will do, that the Father may be glorified in the Son."
JOHN 14:13

"And whatever things you ask in prayer, believing, you will receive."
MATTHEW 21:22

"If you abide in Me, and My words abide in you, you will ask what you desire, and it shall be done for you."
JOHN 15:7

"Call to Me, and I will answer you, and show you great and mighty things, which you do not know."
JEREMIAH 33:3

And whatever we ask we receive from Him, because we keep His commandments and do those things that are pleasing in His sight.
1 JOHN 3:22

Now this is the confidence that we have in Him, that if we ask anything according to His will, He hears us. And if we know that He hears us, whatever we ask, we know that we have the petitions that we have asked of Him.
1 JOHN 5:14–15

IN AN UNCERTAIN WORLD, THE ONE THING I CAN ALWAYS DEPEND ON IS THAT GOD WILL FULFILL HIS PROMISES FOR ME AND MY FAMILY.

Wrong Thinking:

SO OFTEN I WONDER IF I CAN TRUST GOD'S PROMISES.

This hope we have as an anchor of the soul, both sure and steadfast, and which enters the Presence behind the veil. . . .

HEBREWS 6:19

MY FINANCES

GOD WILL FULFILL HIS PROMISES FOR ME AND MY FAMILY

Think about this for a moment: in a world filled with uncertainties and challenges, there is one thing you can always depend on — the faithfulness of our Heavenly Father to fulfill His promises for you and your family. His promises are not empty words; they are the anchor for our souls, sure and steadfast, leading us into His presence and peace.

Scripture reads in Hebrews 6:19, *This hope we have as an anchor of the soul, both sure and steadfast, and which enters the Presence behind the veil. . . .* Our hope in God's promises is not in vain. It is an anchor that holds us firm in the midst of life's storms, leading us into the presence of our loving Father.

In Isaiah 43:26, God tells us, *"Put Me in remembrance; let us contend together; state your case...."* He's telling us to remember His promises, not our problems. You see, it's alright to be transparent and honest with our Heavenly Father. He welcomes your vulnerability. But don't stop at simply recounting your troubles! Elevate your prayers by declaring His promises!

When you pray, don't just recite your laundry list of concerns. Instead, intertwine each challenge with the unshakeable promises of God. When you

do so, you unleash the fullness of His power into your circumstances.

In Numbers 23:19, we're reminded of God's unwavering faithfulness. It says, *"God is not human, that he should lie, not a human being, that he should change his mind. Does he speak and then not act? Does he promise and not fulfill?"* (NIV). Take comfort today in knowing that the God who parted the Red Sea, who raised the dead, who conquered death has never faltered in His promises, and He won't start with you!

Make a decision to anchor your soul in God's promises, no matter what uncertainties may come your way. He will keep His promises, even when circumstances seem bleak. Though His ways may not align with our own and His timing may differ from our expectations, one thing remains true: God is faithful to His Word.

His promises are rooted in His unchanging character and His boundless love for us. As you trust in His promises and lean on His strength, He will guide you through every storm and lead you into His perfect peace.

As you continue to anchor your soul in God's promises, you will experience a newfound sense of confidence. You will walk in the assurance that He is faithful and that nothing can shake the certainty of

Elevate your prayers by declaring His promises!

His promises. So, let us choose to think thoughts of trust and confidence in God's promises, knowing that He will always lead us into His abundant life and everlasting love.

He will guide you through every storm and lead you into His perfect peace.

Power Up✝

I wait for the LORD, my soul waits, and in His word I do hope. My soul waits for the Lord more than those who watch for the morning — yes, more than those who watch for the morning.
PSALM 130:5–6

Through the LORD's mercies we are not consumed, because His compassions fail not. They are new every morning; great is Your faithfulness. "The LORD is my portion," says my soul, "Therefore I hope in Him!" The LORD is good to those who wait for Him, to the soul who seeks Him.
LAMENTATIONS 3:22–25

The LORD is righteous in her midst, He will do no unrighteousness. Every morning He brings His justice to light; He never fails, but the unjust knows no shame.
ZEPHANIAH 3:5

For our light affliction, which is but for a moment, is working for us a far more exceeding and eternal weight of glory, while we do not look at the things which are seen, but at the things which are not seen. For the things which are seen are temporary, but the things which are not seen are eternal.
2 CORINTHIANS 4:17–18

I TRUST GOD TO BLESS ME, BUT MY IDENTITY AND WORTH ARE NOT FOUND IN MATERIAL THINGS.

Wrong Thinking:

I WISH I HAD MORE THINGS.

For He satisfies the longing soul, and fills the hungry soul with goodness.

PSALM 107:9

I TRUST GOD
TO BLESS ME

D o you find yourself wrestling with financial challenges, stuck in the same place, unable to get ahead? Are you adopting a defeated mentality, living like scarcity and struggle define your life? I want to encourage you not to be defined by what you lack but to trust God to bless you and to remind yourself of your true identity in Him. By finding your identity and worth in God, rather than in what you have (or don't have), you will find true satisfaction and fulfillment in God's blessings.

Think about this for a moment: your worth is not determined by the things you possess or the wealth you accumulate. No amount of material possessions can ever truly satisfy the longing of your soul. True satisfaction and fulfillment can only be found in a deep and intimate relationship with our Heavenly Father.

The Bible tells us in Psalm 107:9, *For He satisfies the longing soul, and fills the hungry soul with goodness.* These words are a powerful reminder that true satisfaction and fulfillment come from God alone. He is the source of all good things, and He longs to fill our lives with His goodness and blessings.

When we choose to think thoughts of trusting in God to bless us, while recognizing that our identities and worth are not found in material things, it changes our perspectives. Instead of chasing after fleeting things, we can rest assured in the knowledge that our true worth and identity is created by an eternal God.

In the midst of your trials, start declaring your faith: "I am blessed. I am the head and not the tail. My cup overflows with abundance. Everything I lay my hands upon will prosper."

Do not allow external circumstances to shape your identity. You are abundantly blessed and favored. Where you are doesn't define who you are. Don't be discouraged because time has passed and you haven't seen your prayers answered. You have to stay in faith, keep declaring these truths over yourself, to remind your soul that who you are is not defined by anything on this earth.

True satisfaction and fulfillment can only be found in a deep and intimate relationship with our Heavenly Father.

God has already blessed you in so many ways. Take the time to count your blessings beyond just material things: love, peace, joy, and purpose. Seek His Kingdom first and foremost, and He promises to provide for all your needs according to His riches in glory. Choose to trust in His provision and believe that He will continue to bless you according to His perfect plan.

As you continue to trust in God to bless you, while recognizing that your worth and identity are found in Him alone, you will experience a newfound sense of peace and contentment. You will no longer be driven by the pursuit of worldly wealth but by a desire to know and serve your Heavenly Father. So, let us choose to think thoughts of trust and contentment in God's blessings, knowing that He satisfies the longing soul and fills the hungry soul with goodness.

Choose to trust in His provision and believe that He will continue to bless you according to His perfect plan.

Power Up✛

"Blessed are those who hunger and thirst for righteousness, for they shall be filled."
MATTHEW 5:6

Not that I speak in regard to need, for I have learned in whatever state I am, to be content: I know how to be abased, and I know how to abound. Everywhere and in all things I have learned both to be full and to be hungry, both to abound and to suffer need. I can do all things through Christ who strengthens me.
PHILIPPIANS 4:11–13

How precious is Your lovingkindness, O God! There-fore the children of men put their trust under the shadow of Your wings. They are abundantly satisfied with the fullness of Your house, and You give them drink from the river of Your pleasures.
PSALM 36:7–8

"Ho! Everyone who thirsts, come to the waters; and you who have no money, come, buy and eat. Yes, come, buy wine and milk without money and without price."
ISAIAH 55:1

The young lions lack and suffer hunger; but those who seek the LORD shall not lack any good thing.
PSALM 34:10

Right Thinking:

GOD WILL PROVIDE EVERYTHING I NEED.

Wrong Thinking:

I'M NOT GOING TO HAVE ENOUGH TO PROVIDE FOR MYSELF AND MY FAMILY.

"*The LORD will command the blessing on you in your storehouses and in all to which you set your hand, and He will bless you in the land which the LORD your God is giving you.*"

DEUTERONOMY 28:8

GOD WILL PROVIDE EVERYTHING I NEED

When you look at your circumstances, it may seem like an uphill battle. How can you move forward, achieve your dreams, own your own home, or leave an inheritance for your grandchildren, especially with the challenges today — rising inflation, soaring gas prices, and the increased cost of living? In the natural, it may appear impossible. But God is a supernatural God.

Instead of being consumed with worry about how to provide for yourself and your family, remind yourself of God's promise to provide everything you need. The Bible is filled with promises of God's provision for His children. In Deuteronomy 28:8, we read, *"The LORD will command the blessing on you in your storehouses and in all to which you set your hand, and He will bless you in the land which the LORD your God is giving you."* God's blessings are not limited by our circumstances. He is able to provide for us abundantly.

Philippians 4:19 declares, *And my God shall supply all your need according to His riches in glory by Christ Jesus.* What a powerful reminder! He is not limited by your resources or abilities. His provision flows from His unlimited abundance, and He is able to supply all that you need according to His riches in glory.

Instead of dwelling on feelings of lack and scarcity, we can rest assured that God is working behind the scenes to provide for us. He knows our needs even before we ask, and He is faithful to meet us right where we are. Your words hold tremendous power. They can either breathe life or speak death. You can declare lack, or you can proclaim abundance. You can vocalize scarcity, or you can declare overflow.

Think about Moses. God instructed him to strike a rock with his staff, and what happened? Water gushed forth in the desert — a supernatural provision. That's the kind of God we serve. He has the power to make things happen that defy all odds.

God's blessings are not limited by our circumstances. He is able to provide for us abundantly.

Everything in your mind might be saying that you'll never have enough, you'll always struggle or be in debt. Logically speaking, that may seem true. But let me tell you something: God operates on a different level. He defies logic. He knows how to bring water gushing out of a seemingly barren rock.

Release your worries and fears about provision into God's capable hands. Trust that He sees your needs and cares deeply for you. He is aware of your situation, and He will never leave you nor forsake you. As you place your trust in Him, He will open doors of opportunity, provide for your needs, and bless the work of your hands.

Don't be limited by what you see in the natural. Fix your eyes on the supernatural power of God. Speak words of faith, of abundance, of provision and watch as He works miracles in your life. With God, all things are possible — even bringing water out of a rock. So, dare to believe, to speak life, and to witness God's supernatural provision in your own life. May you experience His blessings overflowing, and may you be a testimony to His goodness and faithfulness to those around you.

Speak words of faith, of abundance, of provision and watch as He works miracles in your life.

Power Up✝

And my God shall supply all your need according to His riches in glory by Christ Jesus.
PHILIPPIANS 4:19

He who did not spare His own Son, but delivered Him up for us all, how shall He not with Him also freely give us all things?
ROMANS 8:32

The young lions lack and suffer hunger; but those who seek the LORD shall not lack any good thing.
PSALM 34:10

"Give, and it will be given to you: good measure, pressed down, shaken together, and running over will be put into your bosom. For with the same measure that you use, it will be measured back to you."
LUKE 6:38

"But seek first the kingdom of God and His righteousness, and all these things shall be added to you."
MATTHEW 6:33

. . . as His divine power has given to us all things that pertain to life and godliness, through the knowledge of Him who called us by glory and virtue. . . .
2 PETER 1:3

21

I AM GOING TO CELEBRATE THE GOOD THINGS THAT HAPPEN TO OTHERS, AND I KNOW GOD HAS GOOD THINGS IN STORE FOR ME TOO.

Wrong Thinking:

I CAN'T BELIEVE THEY HAVE SO MUCH WHILE I HAVE SO LITTLE.

A sound heart is life to the body, but envy is rottenness to the bones.

PROVERBS 14:30

MY FINANCES

CELEBRATE WITH OTHERS

Today is a great day to celebrate the successes and blessings of others. It's easy to fall into the trap of comparison, especially when it seems like others have more than we do. It's easy to look at someone else's success — their new house, their growing family, their big contract — and think, *Why not me? I've been faithful. I've been diligent. I deserve that too.* But I want to encourage you to choose a different mindset.

Scripture teaches us in Proverbs 14:30, *A sound heart is life to the body, but envy is rottenness to the bones.* Think about the destructive nature of envy and comparison. When you allow jealousy to take root in your heart, it not only robs you of joy and contentment but also eats away at your innermost being. Instead of celebrating the blessings of others, you find yourself consumed by bitterness and resentment.

But it doesn't have to be this way. You have the power to choose celebration and trust in God's provision for all. When you choose to celebrate the blessings of others, it changes your perspective on your own circumstances. Instead of dwelling on what you lack, you can rejoice in the abundance that surrounds you and trust that God has good things in store for you too.

Choose to rejoice with those who rejoice, knowing that their victories are a testament to God's faithfulness and provision. Instead of allowing jealousy to creep into your heart, choose to celebrate the goodness of God in others' lives and trust that He has good plans for you.

God's blessings are not limited. He is able to provide for each of us according to His riches in glory. Know that what God has for you is tailor-made, specifically designed to fit you perfectly. If God were to give you something that wasn't meant for you, it wouldn't be a blessing; it would be a burden. You see, you're uniquely anointed for the path that God has laid out for you.

When you choose to celebrate the blessings of others, it changes your perspective on your own circumstances.

God has already lined up the right people, the right opportunities, the right home, the right job, the right promotion — all with your name on it. And let me assure you, nobody can snatch away what God has in store for you.

If you find yourself struggling with feelings of envy or comparison, let your prayer be this: "God, bring me the blessings that You have prepared for me — not for my cousin, not for my friend, not for my neighbor, but for me." Instead of focusing on what others have that you don't, take time to count your own blessings and give thanks for the abundance that surrounds you. Then thank Him in advance for the blessings you haven't seen yet.

As you cultivate a spirit of celebration and gratitude in your heart, you will find that your own joy and contentment will multiply. And as you trust in God's goodness for all, you will experience His blessings in ways you never thought possible. Choose to celebrate the good things that happen to others, knowing that God has good things in store. Trust in His timing, and watch as He pours out abundant blessings — blessings that have your name on them.

Choose to celebrate the good things that happen to others, knowing that God has good things in store.

Power Up⁺

"For wrath kills a foolish man, and envy slays a simple one."
JOB 5:2

Let us walk properly, as in the day, not in revelry and drunkenness, not in lewdness and lust, not in strife and envy.
ROMANS 13:13

He is proud, knowing nothing, but is obsessed with disputes and arguments over words, from which come envy, strife, reviling, evil suspicions. . . .
1 TIMOTHY 6:4

Wrath is cruel and anger a torrent, but who is able to stand before jealousy?
PROVERBS 27:4

Therefore, laying aside all malice, all deceit, hypocrisy, envy, and all evil speaking, as newborn babes, desire the pure milk of the word, that you may grow thereby. . . .
1 PETER 2:1–2

IN DUE TIME . . .

HE WILL BRING FORTH
THE FULLNESS OF
HIS PROMISES!

SCRIPTURES AT A GLANCE

Right Thinking:

I CHOOSE HOPE OVER WORRY, FAITH OVER FEAR.

"Therefore I say to you, do not worry about your life, what you will eat or what you will drink; nor about your body, what you will put on. Is not life more than food and the body more than clothing?" MATTHEW 6:25

Right Thinking:

I KNOW THE LORD IS MAKING A WAY FOR ME EVEN WHEN THERE SEEMS TO BE NO WAY.

But those who wait on the LORD shall renew their strength; they shall mount up with wings like eagles, they shall run and not be weary, they shall walk and not faint. ISAIAH 40:31

Right Thinking:

GOD HAS FREEDOM AND BREAKTHROUGH IN STORE FOR ME.

"My grace is sufficient for you, for My strength is made perfect in weakness." 2 CORINTHIANS 12:9

Right Thinking:

GOD IS WITH ME, I HAVE NOTHING TO FEAR.

Yea, though I walk through the valley of the shadow of death, I will fear no evil; for You are with me; Your rod and Your staff, they comfort me. You prepare a table before me in the presence of my enemies; You anoint my head with oil; my cup runs over. PSALM 23:4–5

Right Thinking:
GOD IS GUIDING MY STEPS, OPENING DOORS OF OPPORTUNITY, LINING UP THE RIGHT CONNECTIONS.
I will instruct you and teach you in the way you should go; I will guide you with My eye. PSALM 32:8

Right Thinking:
GOD CAN HEAL MY HEART AND BRING ME OUT BETTER THAN BEFORE.
The LORD is near to those who have a broken heart, and saves such as have a contrite spirit. PSALM 34:18

Right Thinking:
I'M GOING TO DO WHAT IS RIGHT, REGARDLESS OF WHAT OTHERS DO OR HOW THEY TREAT ME.
And let us not grow weary while doing good, for in due season we shall reap if we do not lose heart. GALATIANS 6:9

Right Thinking:
GOD IS BRINGING THE RIGHT PEOPLE INTO MY LIFE.
Two are better than one, because they have a good reward for their labor. ECCLESIASTES 4:9

Right Thinking:
I REFUSE TO BE HELD BACK BY BITTERNESS AND UNFORGIVENESS. INSTEAD, I CHOOSE TO FORGIVE AND RECEIVE GOD'S HEALING FOR MY SOUL.
Let all bitterness, wrath, anger, clamor, and evil speaking be put away from you, with all malice. And be kind to one another, tenderhearted, forgiving one another, even as God in Christ forgave you. EPHESIANS 4:31–32

Right Thinking:
I CHOOSE TO LIVE MY LIFE HAPPY AND BLOOM WHERE I'M PLANTED. THE JOY OF THE LORD IS MY STRENGTH.

You have put gladness in my heart, more than in the season that their grain and wine increased. PSALM 4:7

Right Thinking:
THERE IS AN ANOINTING OF EASE ON MY LIFE. GOD IS GOING BEFORE ME TO MAKE THE CROOKED PLACES STRAIGHT.

I would have lost heart, unless I had believed that I would see the goodness of the LORD in the land of the living. Wait on the LORD; be of good courage, and He shall strengthen your heart; wait, I say, on the LORD! PSALM 27:13–14

Right Thinking:
I AM THE VERY RIGHTEOUSNESS OF GOD IN CHRIST JESUS. I CAN COME BOLDLY BEFORE HIS THRONE OF GRACE.

He has not dealt with us according to our sins, nor punished us according to our iniquities. For as the heavens are high above the earth, so great is His mercy toward those who fear Him; as far as the east is from the west, so far has He removed our transgressions from us. PSALM 103:10–12

Right Thinking:
GOD CAN DO A "SUDDENLY" MIRACLE IN MY LIFE. HIS TIMING IS PERFECT. I TRUST HIM.

This I recall to my mind, therefore I have hope. Through the LORD's mercies we are not consumed, because His compassions fail not. They are new every morning; great is Your faithfulness. "The LORD is my portion," says my soul, "Therefore I hope in Him!" The LORD is good to those who wait for Him, to the soul who seeks Him. It is good that one should hope and wait quietly for the salvation of the LORD. LAMENTATIONS 3:21–26

NO MATTER HOW I FEEL, I WILL PRAISE GOD AND DECLARE HIS FAITHFULNESS OVER MYSELF AND MY LOVED ONES.

Therefore by Him let us continually offer the sacrifice of praise to God, that is, the fruit of our lips, giving thanks to His name. HEBREWS 13:15

I AM A CHILD OF ALMIGHTY GOD WITH ROYAL DNA RUNNING THROUGH MY VEINS. HE IS A PERFECT FATHER WHO LOVES ME UNCONDITIONALLY.

But God, who is rich in mercy, because of His great love with which He loved us, even when we were dead in trespasses, made us alive together with Christ (by grace you have been saved), and raised us up together, and made us sit together in the heavenly places in Christ Jesus, that in the ages to come He might show the exceeding riches of His grace in His kindness toward us in Christ Jesus. EPHESIANS 2:4–7

I SUBMIT MY LIFE TO GOD'S WORD AND HIS PURPOSES FOR ME.

"Blessed is the man who trusts in the LORD, and whose hope is in the LORD." JEREMIAH 17:7

Right Thinking:

NOT ONLY DOES GOD HEAR MY PRAYER, BUT HE IS ALREADY MAKING A WAY FOR ME. I MAY NOT SEE IT YET, BUT I'M GOING TO STAY IN FAITH, TRUSTING HIS PROMISES.

The LORD is near to all who call upon Him, to all who call upon Him in truth. He will fulfill the desire of those who fear Him; He also will hear their cry and save them. PSALM 145:18–19

Right Thinking:

IN AN UNCERTAIN WORLD, THE ONE THING I CAN ALWAYS DEPEND ON IS THAT GOD WILL FULFILL HIS PROMISES FOR ME AND MY FAMILY.

This hope we have as an anchor of the soul, both sure and steadfast, and which enters the Presence behind the veil. . . . HEBREWS 6:19

Right Thinking:

I TRUST GOD TO BLESS ME, BUT MY IDENTITY AND WORTH ARE NOT FOUND IN MATERIAL THINGS.

For He satisfies the longing soul, and fills the hungry soul with goodness. PSALM 107:9

Right Thinking:

GOD WILL PROVIDE EVERYTHING I NEED.

"The LORD will command the blessing on you in your storehouses and in all to which you set your hand, and He will bless you in the land which the LORD your God is giving you." DEUTERONOMY 28:8

Right Thinking:

I AM GOING TO CELEBRATE THE GOOD THINGS THAT HAPPEN TO OTHERS, AND I KNOW GOD HAS GOOD THINGS IN STORE FOR ME TOO.

A sound heart is life to the body, but envy is rottenness to the bones. PROVERBS 14:30

Stay encouraged *and* inspired all through the week.

Download the Joel Osteen Daily Podcast *and* subscribe now *on* YouTube to get the latest videos.

For a full listing, visit **JoelOsteen.com/How-To-Watch**.

Stay connected, *be* blessed.

Get more from Joel & Victoria Osteen

It's time to step into the life of victory and favor that God has planned for you! Featuring new messages from Joel & Victoria Osteen, their free daily devotional, and inspiring articles, hope is always at your fingertips with the free Joel Osteen app and online at JoelOsteen.com.

Get the app and visit us today at JoelOsteen.com.

CONNECT WITH US